Pakistani

Recipes

Authentic Pakistani Dishes to Die for

BY

Rachael Rayner

License Notes

No part of this Book can be reproduced in any form or by any means including print, electronic, scanning or photocopying unless prior permission is granted by the author.

All ideas, suggestions and guidelines mentioned here are written for informative purposes. While the author has taken every possible step to ensure accuracy, all readers are advised to follow information at their own risk. The author cannot be held responsible for personal and/or commercial damages in case of misinterpreting and misunderstanding any part of this Book

Table of Contents

Introduction

The diversified culture of Pakistan is very much vivid in their cooking too. The different towns have different dishes to offer. Pakistanis have a love for food but they do not waste any food. You will see them using fish head, fish eggs, leftover meat for breakfast the next etc. Pakistanis are quite health conscious too.

Although they enjoy food, they know how to balance things. They love rice but do not have rice every single day. Rice dishes like Biriyani is made during special occasions. They eat tortillas three times a day. They love their meat, but they plan their everyday meals around vegetables too. You will find several veggie dishes in the book that are finger-licking good.

The book caters to both non-vegetarians and vegetarians. The use of ginger is very prominent as it helps to digest our food and it good for our body. They love spicy food so a lot of chilies and red chili powder are used. Try making these recipes at home and find out which one you like the most.

Potato Lentil Cauliflower Curry

Pakistanis love their curries. They love their vegetables too. Adding lentils to veggies adds a different texture and more flavors to the curries.

Serving Size: 4

Cooking Time: 30 Minutes

Ingredients:

- 1 cup diced potatoes
- 1 cup diced cauliflower
- 1 cup lentil, soaked
- 2 cup vegetable stock
- Fresh coriander, chopped
- 2 green chilies
- 2 tbsp mustard oil
- Salt to taste
- 1 tsp red chili powder
- 1tsp cumin
- 1 tsp coriander powder
- ½ tsp black cumin seeds

Instruction

In a pressure cooker, heat the oil and fry the black cumin seeds for a minute.

Add the lentil. Add 1 cup of vegetable stock. Cover and cook for 10 minutes with a lid.

Add the veggies, spices, salt and green chilies. Pour in the rest of the stock.

Cover again. Cook for 20 minutes. Serve hot.

Chapli Kabob or Chicken fried Kabob

Chapli kabob is very famous in Pakistan. It is found in both street food courts and in fancy restaurants. The price tag is different in two places but the authentic taste is quite the same. You can make it at home too.

Serving Size: 2

Cooking Time: 20 Minutes

Ingredients:

- 2 chicken breasts, skinless, boneless
- 2 tbsp corn flour
- 2 tbsp rice flour
- Pepper to taste
- Fresh scallion, chopped, to serve
- 1 tsp ginger garlic paste
- 1 tsp vinegar
- 2 tbsp mustard oil
- Salt to taste
- 1 tsp red chili powder
- 1tsp cumin

Instruction

Combine the spices, vinegar, ginger garlic paste, salt, and pepper.

Mix well and add the flours. Mix again.

Flatten the chicken breasts using kitchen hammer.

Marinate the chicken pieces in the flour mixture for 2 hours.

In a pan heat the oil. Fry the chicken kabobs for 5 minutes on each side. The color should be brown. Serve hot with chopped scallions on top.

Carrot Peas Papaya Curry

As mentioned before, Pakistanis love their vegetables as much as they love meat. This is one of their veggie recipes that usually eaten at breakfast or as a side dish with rice or tortilla.

Serving Size: 2

Cooking Time: 20 Minutes

Ingredients:

- 1 cup diced raw papaya
- 1 cup diced carrot
- ½ cup peas
- 2 cup water
- Fresh coriander, chopped, to serve
- 2 green chilies
- 1 tbsp mustard oil
- Salt to taste
- 1 tsp red chili powder
- 1tsp cumin
- 1 tsp coriander powder

Instruction

Prepare the veggies and wash them properly.

In a wok, heat the oil. Fry the onion for 1 minute.

Add the veggies and stir for 2 minutes.

Add the cumin, salt, red chili powder, and coriander powder.

Toss for 5 minutes. Add the chilies, water and cover.

Cook on high heat for 10 minutes. Serve hot with fresh coriander on top.

Ghee Naan Ruti or Tortilla

Pakistanis staple in the kitchen is tortillas; they eat it in breakfast, lunch and dinner. There are various types of tortillas they eat. This is one of their festive tortilla recipes.

Serving Size: 4

Cooking Time: 10 Minutes

Ingredients:

- 2 cup all purpose flour
- A pinch of salt
- 1 cup water
- 4 tbsp ghee for frying

Instruction

In a pot heat the water. Add the salt.

When the water starts to a boil add the flour. Mix well. Turn off the heat.

Knead using your hands. Divide dough into 10 balls.

Roll out as thin as you can for each ball.

Fry them with ghee from both sides. Serve with any curry of your choice.

Keema Matar or Minced Beef with Peas

Keema matar is a traditional Pakistani recipe that tastes finger-licking good. You will be surprised to know it takes only 20 minutes to cook. It is usually served with rice.

Serving Size: 2

Cooking Time: 20 Minutes

Ingredients:

- 1 cup peas
- 1 cup minced beef
- 1 cup chopped onion
- 1 cinnamon stick
- 2 black cardamom
- 2 green chilies, chopped
- 1 tbsp mustard oil
- Salt to taste
- 1 tsp red chili powder
- 1tsp cumin
- 1 tsp coriander powder

Instruction

In a wok, heat the oil. Add the minced beef.

Add the cumin, red chili powder, coriander, salt, black cardamom and cinnamon stick.

Stir for 6 minutes and add the peas and onion.

Add the green chilies and stir continuously for 10 minutes.

Serve hot.

Cottage cheese with Spinach Curry

This is another authentic Pakistani Vegetarian dish. The cottage cheese in the recipe adds so much more flavors to this vegetarian dish. You can use any greens of your choice but traditionally it is made with spinach.

Serving Size: 2

Cooking Time: 15 Minutes

Ingredients:

- 1 cup cubed firm cottage cheese
- 1 cup diced spinach
- Fresh coriander, chopped
- ½ tsp turmeric
- 2 green chilies
- 1 tbsp mustard oil
- ½ tsp red chili powder
- 2 red onion, diced
- 4 garlic cloves, chopped
- Salt to taste
- 1tsp cumin
- 1 tsp coriander powder

Instruction

In a skillet heat the mustard oil.

Add the onion. Cook for 2 minutes.

Add the cumin, coriander powder, salt, garlic, red chili powder, turmeric and stir for 1 minute.

Add the cottage cheese and cook until they become golden in color.

Add the spinach and stir well.

Cover with lid and cook on low heat for 5 minutes.

Add the chilies and cook for another minute. Serve hot.

Okra Stir Fry

Okra is very good for the body and skin. Pakistanis know its health value and enjoy this green veggie in the form of stir fry. Although, they like it slightly crispy!

Serving Size: 2

Cooking Time: 10 Minutes

Ingredients:

- 2 cup sliced okra
- Fresh coriander, chopped
- 2 green chilies cut in half
- 1 tbsp mustard oil
- Salt to taste
- A pinch of turmeric
- 1tsp cumin
- 1 red onion, chopped
- ½ tsp black cumin seeds

Instruction

In a wok, heat the mustard oil and add the black cumin seeds.

Toss for 30 seconds and add the onion. Fry the onion until brown.

Add the okra. Toss for 2 minutes. Add the salt, cumin, green chilies, turmeric, and stir for 5 minutes.

Add the coriander and cook for another 3 minutes.

Serve hot with rice.

Tangy Chicken Saslick or skewers

Pakistanis love their kabobs and skewers. They make it quite often. This recipe can be made very easily and takes about less than 15 minutes cooking time. So you can make it conveniently at any time.

Serving Size: 2

Cooking Time: 15 Minutes

Ingredients:

- 2 chicken breasts
- 1 tbsp vinegar
- 1 tbsp lemon juice
- 1 tsp ginger paste
- 1 tsp garlic paste
- 2 tbsp mustard oil
- 1 tsp sugar
- Salt to taste
- 1 tsp red chili powder
- Black pepper to taste

Instruction

Discard the chicken breast's skin and bones. Cut into cubes.

In a bowl mix the salt, sugar, pepper, lemon juice, vinegar, red chili powder, ginger and garlic paste.

Mix well and add the chicken cubes. Marinate for 1 hour or so.

Thread the chicken cubes into skewers.

In a pan heat the mustard oil. Fry each side of the skewers for 5 minutes.

Serve hot with lemon wedges on the side.

Chicken Biriyani or Pakistani Chicken Rice

Pakistanis love Biriyani. Biriyani is a rice dish which has meat or vegetables in it. It has a strong aroma from all the spices used. Usually yogurt is used to marinate the meat.

Serving Size: 4

Cooking Time: 1 hour

Ingredients:

- 3 cup long grain rice
- 1 cup diced potatoes
- 4 lemon slices
- 1 cup diced tomatoes
- 2 lb. chicken, cut into medium pieces
- ½ tsp turmeric
- 1 cup yogurt
- 2 tbsp ginger garlic paste
- Fresh coriander, chopped
- 2 bay leaves
- 4 green chilies
- 4 tbsp mustard oil
- Salt to taste
- 2 tsp red chili powder
- 2 cinnamon stick
- 2 tsp cumin
- 2 tsp coriander powder
- 2 tbsp lemon juice
- Pepper to taste
- 2 star anise

Instruction

Cook the rice for 8 minutes with salted water. Drain well and set aside for now.

Combine the ginger garlic paste, yogurt, lemon juice, cumin, coriander powder, red chili powder, salt, pepper, and marinate the chicken in it for 2 hours.

In a large nonstick pot, add the oil. Add the onion, bay leaves, star anise, cinnamon stick and toss for 2 minutes.

Add the chicken and potatoes. Add the rice on top. Add the tomatoes, coriander and green chilies.

Cover with the lid and cook for 1 hour at low heat.

Stir well before serving.

Pan Fried Cauliflower

Cauliflower is eaten quite often in Pakistani cuisine. They enjoy different forms of this vegetable. This recipe makes the cauliflower roasted with aromatic spices and lemon flavors.

Serving Size: 2

Cooking Time: 20 Minutes

Ingredients:

- 1 cup diced cauliflower
- 1 cup red onion, sliced
- 6-8 lemon slices
- ½ cup vegetable stock
- Fresh coriander, chopped
- 1 dried red chili, chopped
- 2 tbsp mustard oil
- Salt to taste
- Pepper to taste
- 1 tsp red chili powder
- 1tsp cumin
- A pinch of cumin seeds
- A pinch of fenugreek seeds

Instruction

Discard the stem of the cauliflower. Dice the florets into medium chunks.

In a pan add the mustard oil and heat over medium heat.

Add the dried red chili, onion and cook until they are golden.

Add the cauliflower. Toss for 2 minutes.

Add all the rest of the ingredients.

Stir for 10 minutes. Serve hot with a dipping sauce and tortilla.

Gingery Lemony Mutton

You will lick your finger if you try making this dish. It tastes so good. The meat is juicy and has a very soft texture to it. The zesty lemon and strong flavors of ginger complements each other.

Serving Size: 2

Cooking Time: 20 Minutes

Ingredients:

- 2 lb. mutton
- 1 lemon, cut into thin slices
- 2 tbsp lemon juice
- ½ tsp turmeric
- 1 tomato, diced
- 2 tbsp thinly chopped ginger
- 2 cup mutton broth
- Fresh coriander, chopped
- 4 green chilies
- 4 tbsp mustard oil
- Salt to taste
- 2 tsp red chili powder
- 2 tbsp tomato sauce
- 1 tbsp ginger paste
- 1 tbsp garlic paste
- 2 tsp cumin
- 3 tsp coriander powder

Instruction

Cut the mutton into bite size pieces. Keep the bones intact.

In a large pan, heat the mustard oil.

Add the chopped ginger and toss for 1 minute.

Add the ginger garlic paste, spices and 2 tbsp broth.

Cook for 5 minutes. Add the mutton and stir. Cover and cook for 20 minutes.

Add the tomato, chilies, rest of the broth and lemon slices.

Cover again and cook for 30 minutes. Add the lemon juice and coriander. Stir well and serve hot.

Spicy Keema Fry or Minced Mutton Fry

Pakistanis love their minced meat dishes. This one is made from minced mutton and it takes less than 20 minutes to prepare. It can be served with tortilla.

Serving Size: 2

Cooking Time: 20 Minutes

Ingredients:

- 1 lb. minced mutton
- 2 jalapeno pepper, chopped
- 1 tbsp chopped ginger
- 1 star anise
- 1 cinnamon stick
- 1 bay leaf
- ½ cup mutton broth
- Fresh coriander, chopped, to serve
- 1 black cardamom
- 1 tbsp mustard oil
- Salt to taste
- Red chili powder to taste

Instruction

In a wok, add the oil. Add the cinnamon, bay leaf, cardamom, star anise and ginger.

Toss for 2 minutes. Add the minced mutton. Stir for 5 minutes.

Add the salt, red chili powder and mutton broth.

Cook on high heat for 10 minutes. Add the jalapeno pepper and coriander.

Cook for 2 more minutes and serve hot.

Mutton Curry

Pakistanis make mutton curry when there is a special occasion. If there is a party or a family gathering, mutton curry is a must dish in their menu.

Serving Size: 2

Cooking Time: 20 Minutes

Ingredients:

- 2 lb. mutton
- 6 cup water
- Fresh coriander, chopped
- ½ tsp turmeric
- 6 green chilies cut in half
- ½ cup mustard oil
- 6 garlic cloves, minced
- 2 inch ginger root, thinly sliced
- Salt to taste
- 3 tsp red chili powder
- 3 cinnamon stick
- 4 cardamoms
- 3 bay leaves
- 4 tbsp ginger garlic paste
- 1 cup diced onion
- 2 tsp cumin
- 3 tsp coriander powder

Instruction

Keep the bones of the mutton. Cut the mutton into bite size pieces.

In a pressure cooker, add the oil. Add the mutton and sear for 5 minutes.

Add the spices, pastes, onion, ginger, garlic, and cover.

Cook for 15 minutes. Add the water. Stir well. Cover again.

Cook for 20 minutes. Add the green chilies, coriander and stir. Cook for another 20 minutes.

Serve hot with sliced ginger on top.

Meatballs in Coconut Gravy

Meatballs tastes good by itself but when you make a coconut gravy to go with it, it becomes heavenly delicious. This is one of Pakistan's signature dish!

Serving Size: 4

Cooking Time: 30 Minutes

Ingredients:

- 2 eggs
- 2 cup coconut milk
- 1 cup heavy cream
- 2 cup minced beef
- Fresh coriander, chopped
- ½ tsp turmeric
- 2 green chilies, chopped
- 1 tsp paprika
- 1 tbsp mustard oil
- Salt to taste
- 1 tsp red chili powder
- 2 tbsp ginger garlic paste
- 1 cup diced white onion

Instruction

In a bowl combine the minced beef with the eggs.

Add the green chilies, chopped onion, salt and paprika.

Mix well and create meatballs. Fry them golden brown.

In another pan, heat the oil. Add the ginger garlic paste.

Stir for 30 seconds. Add the rest of the spices. Add the coconut milk.

Cook for 10 minutes. Add the meatballs. Cook for 10 minutes.

Add the heavy cream. Check the seasoning. Add the green chilies, and coriander.

Cook for 5 minutes on high heat. Serve hot.

Fish with Tomato Curry

Pakistanis enjoy eating fish too. Adding tomatoes with it makes the dish quite interesting.

Serving Size: 4

Cooking Time: 20 Minutes

Ingredients:

- 4 fish fillets
- 1 cup diced tomatoes
- 1 cup water
- Fresh coriander, chopped
- 4 green chilies
- 3 tbsp mustard oil
- Salt to taste
- 1 tsp red chili powder
- 1 tsp turmeric
- 1 tbsp ginger garlic paste
- 2 onion, chopped
- 1tsp cumin
- 1 tsp coriander powder

Instruction

Sprinkle some salt, red chili powder and turmeric onto the fish.

In a pan, heat the oil. Fry the fish for 2 minutes on each side. Transfer to a plate.

In the same pan, add the chopped onion. Cook for 1 minute.

Add the turmeric, red chili powder, cumin, coriander powder and ginger garlic paste.

Add 2 tbsp water and cook for 3 minutes. Add the tomatoes and cook for 3 minutes.

Pour in the water and bring it to boil. Add the fried fish and green chilies.

Cook for 10 minutes. Add the coriander and serve hot.

Potato Stir Fry

This is a simple vegetarian Pakistani dish that you will find in most household almost every single day.

Serving Size: 2

Cooking Time: 20 Minutes

Ingredients:

- 2 cup diced potatoes
- 1 tsp chili flakes
- Fresh coriander, chopped
- 2 green chilies
- 1 tbsp mustard oil
- Salt to taste
- 1 white onion, chopped
- 2 garlic cloves, minced
- 1tsp cumin
- ½ tsp black cumin seeds

Instruction

In a wok, heat the mustard oil. Add the black cumin seeds and cook for only 20 seconds.

Add the chopped onion and the minced garlic. Cook for 2 minutes.

Add the diced potatoes. Cook for 2 minutes. Add the salt, cumin, green chilies and chili flakes.

Cook for 5 minutes and stir. Cook for another 5 minutes and stir.

Add the coriander and take off the heat. Serve with tortilla.

Spicy Chickpeas

Pakistanis enjoys legumes too and amongst legumes, chickpeas are one of their favorites. There are many way you can make chickpeas, this one is slightly a healthy Pakistani chickpea recipe.

Serving Size: 2

Cooking Time: 30 Minutes

Ingredients:

- 1 cup chickpeas
- 1 cup chopped tomatoes
- 2 green chilies, chopped
- 1 tsp olive oil
- Salt to taste
- Pepper to taste
- Paprika to taste
- Red chili powder to taste
- 1 tbsp lemon juice
- 1 tsp minced ginger

Instruction

In a pressure cooker boil the chickpeas with water for 30 minutes.

Drain and rinse off well.

In a mixing bowl combine the onion, tomato, green chilies, ginger, lemon juice, and chickpeas.

Add the seasoning and spices. Mix well and serve.

Paya or Nihari or Leg Stew

Pakistanis love their meat leg stew. It is a runny broth made with mutton leg or beef leg. The dish is very liquid like and is very high on calcium. So, anyone suffering from bone density should try this.

Serving Size: 4

Cooking Time: 1 hour

Ingredients:

- 2 lb. mutton legs, cut into medium pieces
- 8 cup water
- Fresh coriander, chopped, to serve
- 2 peppercorns
- 2 star anise
- 2 bread slices
- 2 green chilies
- 2 tbsp mustard oil
- Salt to taste
- 1 tsp red chili powder
- 1 cinnamon stick
- 2 cardamoms
- 2 bay leaves
- 1 tsp ginger garlic paste
- 1 cup diced white onion
- 1tsp cumin
- 1 tsp coriander powder

Instruction

In a pressure cooker, add the oil, onion, star anise, peppercorn, coriander, cumin, ginger garlic paste, cardamom, bay leaves, cinnamon, red chili paste, and water.

Add the mutton and stir. Cover and cook for 40 minutes on low heat.

Soak the bread pieces in milk and crumble using your hands.

Add to the pressure cooker. Add the green chilies and cook for another 20 minutes.

Serve hot with coriander on top.

One Pot Mutton Biriyani

Mutton Biriyani is more authentic than other meat biriyani Pakistanis have. Originally this biriyani dish was meant to be made with mutton and layer people found different variations to make it with chicken, beef, fish etc.

Serving Size: 4

Cooking Time: 1 hour

Ingredients:

- 2 cup long grain rice
- 2 lb. mutton, cut into medium pieces
- ½ tsp turmeric
- 1 cup yogurt
- 2 tbsp ginger garlic paste
- 2 bay leaves
- ½ tsp saffron, mixed with 3 tbsp warm water
- 4 green chilies
- 4 tbsp mustard oil
- Salt to taste
- 2 tbsp clarified butter
- 2 tsp red chili powder
- 2 cinnamon stick
- 2 tsp cumin
- 2 tsp coriander powder
- 2 tbsp lemon juice
- Pepper to taste
- 2 star anise

Instruction

Marinate the mutton with star anise, lemon juice, pepper, coriander, cumin, cinnamon, salt, red chili powder, mustard oil, bay leaves, ginger garlic paste, yogurt, turmeric and mix well. Let it sit overnight.

Take a deep dish pot and add the marinated mutton with all the juice.

Add the soaked rice on top. Add some salt on top. Add the saffron mix. Add the clarified butter.

Cover with lid. Cook on low heat for 40 minutes. Stir once. Cook with the lid on for another 20 minutes. Serve hot.

Pakistani Scorch Eggs

This is a wonderful egg dish that uses minced meat as a coating for the egg. The gravy is made from tamarind and tomatoes. It is quite a unique dish.

Serving Size: 4

Cooking Time: 30 Minutes

Ingredients:

- 5 eggs
- 2 cup minced beef
- 1 cup vegetable stock
- 2 tbsp tomato sauce
- 1tsp cumin
- 1 tbsp soy sauce
- Fresh coriander, chopped
- 2 green chilies cut in half
- 2 tbsp mustard oil
- Salt to taste
- Pepper to taste
- 1 tsp coriander powder
- 1 tsp red chili powder
- 2 tbsp ginger garlic paste
- 1 cup diced white onion

Instruction

Hard boil 4 eggs in salted water for 8 minutes. Drain and add cold water on top.

Remove the shells. Combine the minced beef with salt, pepper and 1 egg. Wrap each egg in the beef mixture.

Fry them golden brown. Set aside for now.

In a pan, heat the mustard oil. Fry the onion for 1 minute.

Add the ginger garlic paste and 1 tbsp of water. Cook for 1 minute.

Add all the spices, tomato sauce and soy sauce. Add some salt and pepper.

Pour in the vegetable stock. Bring it to boil. Simmer for 5 minutes.

Add the fried eggs and green chilies. Cook for 5 minutes. Add coriander on top and serve.

Vegetable One Pot Biriyani

If you are craving for Biriyani but do not want to eat meat, you can try this delicious vegetarian biriyani.

Serving Size: 2

Cooking Time: 40 Minutes

Ingredients:

- 2 cup basmati rice
- 1cup Bengal grams
- 10 cashews
- 2 tsp red chili powder
- 1 cup diced cauliflower
- 1 cup diced potatoes
- ½ tsp saffron, mixed with 3 tbsp warm water
- 1 cup tofu, cut into cubes
- ½ tsp turmeric
- 1 cup yogurt
- 2 tbsp ginger garlic paste
- 2 bay leaves
- 4 green chilies
- 2 tbsp lemon juice
- 4 tbsp mustard oil
- 2 cinnamon stick
- Salt to taste
- 2 tbsp clarified butter
- 2 tsp cumin
- 2 tsp coriander powder
- Pepper to taste
- 1 star anise

Instruction

Marinate the vegetables, Bengal gram and tofu with star anise, lemon juice, pepper, coriander, cumin, cinnamon, salt, red chili powder, mustard oil, bay leaves, ginger garlic paste, yogurt, turmeric and mix well.

Keep it marinating for 30 minutes.

In a large pot, add the veggie mix.

Add the soaked rice on top. Add the clarified butter, salt and saffron mix.

Cover with lid. Cook on low heat for 20 minutes. Stir once. Cook with the lid on for another 10 minutes. Serve hot.

Chickpea Curry

The earthy flavor of curry leaves and the sweetness of the tomatoes and bay leaves makes this chickpea curry unforgettable.

Serving Size: 2

Cooking Time: 1 hour

Ingredients:

- 2 cup chickpeas, soaked
- ½ cup tomatoes, chopped
- 2 cup vegetable stock
- Fresh coriander, chopped
- 1 green chili
- 1 red chili
- 1 tsp cumin
- 1 tsp curry leaves
- 2 tbsp mustard oil
- Salt to taste
- 1 tsp red chili powder
- 2 bay leaves
- 1 tbsp ginger garlic paste
- 1 onion, diced

Instruction

In a pan heat the oil. Add the onion, then cook for 1 minute.

Add the ginger garlic paste and cook for 1 minute.

Add the bay leaves, curry leaves and spices.

Add in the chickpeas and cook for 3 minutes. Add the stock.

Cover and cook for 25 minutes on high heat.

Add the chilies, tomatoes, coriander and salt.

Cook for another 30 minutes. Serve hot.

Haleem or Meat Legume Curry

Pakistanis love Haleem. This is a curry made with mutton or beef meat combined with different types of legumes like Bengal gram, mung bean, and lentil.

Serving Size: 2

Cooking Time: 20 Minutes

Ingredients:

- 1 cup diced mutton pieces, with bones and fat
- ½ cup red lentil
- 2 tbsp rice
- ½ cup Bengal gram
- 6 cup water
- 2 tbsp mustard oil
- Salt to taste
- 1 tsp red chili powder
- 1 cup diced white onion
- 1tsp cumin
- 1 tsp coriander powder
- 4 peppercorns
- 2 tbsp ginger garlic paste
- 3 cloves
- 2 tbsp sliced ginger, to serve
- Fresh coriander, chopped, to serve
- 2 green chilies, chopped, to serve

Instruction

Soak the legumes and rice in water overnight. Drain well and wash well.

In a pressure cooker, add the oil, onion, mutton, ginger garlic paste, cloves, peppercorns, cumin, red chili powder, coriander powder, salt and water.

Cover and cook for 20 minutes. Add the rice, and legume.

Add the water. Cook for 30 minutes. Serve hot with chilies, coriander and ginger on top.

Kemaa Shabji or Minced meat with Potatoes and Peas

As mentioned earlier, Pakistanis love their minced beef. Here the recipe combines minced beef with potatoes and peas. Both complement the minced beef very well.

Serving Size: 2

Cooking Time: 30 Minutes

Ingredients:

- 1 cup diced potatoes
- 1 cup peas
- 1 cup minced beef
- 1 cup vegetable stock
- Fresh coriander, chopped
- 2 green chilies cut in half
- Salt to taste
- 2 tbsp mustard oil
- 1 tsp coriander powder
- 2 tbsp ginger garlic paste
- 1 tsp red chili powder
- ½ cup diced onion
- 1tsp cumin
- 1/3 tsp turmeric
- ½ tsp black cumin seeds

Instruction

In a large wok, heat the oil. Add the onion and black cumin seeds.

Toss for 2 minutes. Add the minced beef and toss for 2 minutes.

Add the spices, ginger garlic paste, salt, and other veggies.

Cook for 10 minutes. Add the coriander and green chilies. Cook for 3 minutes.

Serve hot with rice or tortilla.

Spicy Gingery Beef and Potato Curry

Beef and potatoes go really well together. Adding the sliced ginger is to make your digestion quicker.

Serving Size: 4

Cooking Time: 1 hour

Ingredients:

- 1 cup diced potatoes
- 2 lb. beef, boneless, cut into medium chunks
- 4 cup water
- 2 green chilies
- 2 tbsp mustard oil
- Salt to taste
- 2 cardamoms
- 2 tsp red chili powder
- 1 tsp turmeric
- 2 bay leaves
- 2 tbsp ginger garlic paste
- 1 cup diced onion
- 2tsp cumin
- 1 cinnamon stick
- 3 tsp coriander powder
- Fresh coriander, chopped, to serve
- 1 tbsp sliced ginger, to serve
- 1 tsp roasted cumin powder, to serve
- Black pepper to serve

Instruction

Combine all the spices, oil, ginger garlic paste, and marinate the beef in it for 4 hours.

In a pressure cooker, add the beef with its juice.

Cover and cook for 30 minutes.

Add the potatoes, water, and green chilies. Cook for 30 minutes.

Serve hot with ginger, coriander, roasted cumin and black pepper on top.

Cashew Chicken Curry

Chicken curry is good but cashew chicken curry is heavenly! This dish is prepared during special occasions like wedding or Eid or family get together.

Serving Size: 4

Cooking Time: 40 Minutes

Ingredients:

- 2 lb. chicken, cut into bite size pieces, boneless
- 2 cup cashew milk
- 10 cashew nuts, roasted, to serve
- Fresh coriander, chopped, to serve
- 2 green chilies
- 2 tbsp sunflower oil
- Salt to taste
- White pepper to taste
- 2 tbsp cashew paste
- 1 tsp red chili powder
- 1 pinch of turmeric
- 1 cinnamon stick
- 2 cardamoms
- 2 bay leaves
- 2 tbsp ginger garlic paste
- 2 large white onion, chopped

Instruction

In a large pan, heat the oil. Fry the chicken pieces golden brown.

Transfer the chicken onto a plate for now.

Add the onion and cook for 3 minutes.

Add all ginger garlic paste, cashew paste and the spices. Add 2 tbsp water and mix well.

Cover and cook for 5 minutes. Add the chicken and stir well. Cook for 10 minutes.

Pour in the cashew milk and green chilies. Cook on high heat for 15 minutes.

Serve hot with coriander, and cashews on top.

Chicken Karai or Spicy Chicken Curry

Serving Size: 2

Cooking Time: 20 Minutes

Ingredients:

- 2 lb. chicken, cut into bite size pieces
- ½ cup water
- 2 tbsp mustard oil
- Salt to taste
- 1 tsp red chili powder
- 2 bay leaves
- 1 tsp turmeric
- 1 cinnamon stick
- Fresh coriander, chopped
- 4 green chilies
- 1tsp cumin
- 2 cardamoms
- 2 tbsp ginger garlic paste
- 1 cup chopped onion
- 1 tsp coriander powder
- ½ tsp black cumin seeds
- ½ tsp cumin seeds

Instruction

In a wok, heat the mustard oil and add the cumin seeds and black cumin seeds.

Toss for 1 minute and add the onion. Cook until they become brown.

Add the chicken and toss for 5 minutes.

Add the cinnamon, bay leaves, cardamom, turmeric, cumin, coriander powder, red chili powder and salt.

Add 2 tbsp of water and cook for 10 minutes. Add the chilies, coriander and water.

Cook for 20 minutes. Keep stirring continuously. Serve hot.

Matar Polao or Pea Rice

This dish again shows how peas and biriyani is loved by the Pakistanis. This is a vegetarian biriyani made with only peas and onion. But you would be surprised how well it tastes.

Serving Size: 2

Cooking Time: 20 Minutes

Ingredients:

- 1 cup diced red onion
- 2 cup basmati rice
- 2 tbsp clarified butter
- 4 cup water
- 1 cup peas
- 2 green chilies
- 2 tbsp mustard oil
- Salt to taste
- 1 tsp red chili powder
- 1 cinnamon stick
- 2 cardamoms
- 1 tbsp rose water
- 2 bay leaves
- 2 tbsp ginger garlic paste

Instruction

In a pot, heat the mustard oil. Fry the onion golden brown.

Transfer the onion to a kitchen towel.

Add all the spices and ginger garlic paste in the same pot,

Cook for 2 minutes. Add the rice and peas.

Add salt and toss for 5 minutes on low heat.

Pour in the water and cover. Cook on high heat for 10 minutes.

Add the golden brown onion, clarified butter and rose water on top.

Cover and cook on low heat for 15 minutes. Stir well and combine everything together. Serve hot.

Keema Roti or Meat Stuffed Tortilla

This dish tastes even better than it looks. You can use any meat of your choice but popularly in Pakistan, beef is used to make this dish.

Serving Size: 4

Cooking Time: 30 Minutes

Ingredients:

For the Tortilla:

- 2 cup all purpose flour
- A pinch of salt
- 1 cup water
- 2 tbsp oil

For the Filling:

- 2 cup minced beef
- 1 cup chopped tomatoes
- Salt to taste
- 4 garlic cloves, minced
- 2 inch ginger, minced
- 1 cup shredded cabbage
- Fresh coriander, chopped
- 2 tbsp clarified butter
- 2 green chilies, chopped
- 1 cup diced white onion
- 1tsp cumin
- Pepper to taste
- 1 tsp red chili powder
- 1 pinch of cinnamon powder

- 1 tsp coriander powder
- 2 tbsp ginger garlic paste

Instruction

Combine the water, flour, salt and oil together.

Make dough and let it sit for 30 minutes. Divide them into 20 balls.

Let them sit for another 30 minutes. Meanwhile work on the filling. In a pan add the oil and fry the minced beef for 3 minutes.

Add all the spices, herbs, chilies and cabbage. Add salt and pepper, ginger garlic paste and cook for 5 minutes. Add the tomatoes and cook for 5 minutes. Take off the heat.

Now roll out each dough ball into flat tortilla. Layer the minced beef mix on top generously.

Add another tortilla on top and seal the edges carefully.

Repeat with the rest of the ingredients. Fry the tortillas golden brown with clarified butter.

Dahi Bara or Mung Bean with Yogurt

Although it looks like a dessert but it is actually a snack very popular in Pakistan. They enjoy it during the hot days as the yogurt helps them to calm their nerves during summer. Mung bean is used to make falafel and then it is soaked in yogurt. Tamarind sauce is added on top.

Serving Size: 4

Cooking Time: 30 Minutes

Ingredients:

For the falafel:

- 2 cup soaked mung bean
- ½ cup rice, soaked
- Fresh coriander, chopped
- 2 green chilies, chopped
- Salt to taste
- Pepper to taste
- Paprika to taste
- 1 cup diced white onion
- ½ tsp cumin
- ½ tsp coriander powder
- Oil for frying
- Sweet yogurt, to serve
- Mint leaves, to serve
- Tamarind sauce, to serve

Instruction

In a blender add the rice, mung bean and blend until properly smooth.

In a bowl add the mixture. Add in the onion, chilies, coriander, cumin, coriander powder, salt, pepper and paprika.

Create little balls using your hands and fry them golden brown with oil.

Let them cool down slightly.

Add them in a bowl of yogurt. Let them soak for 4 hours.

Sprinkle some salt, pepper, and paprika on top. Add mint leaves on top and serve.

Conclusion

Pakistani cuisine is not your average cuisine. Their food is versatile and gives curiosity to any foodie to try their dishes themselves. Even if you have never visited the country, you can get an idea of their culture by plunging into the type of food they eat. The sweet and savory taste of their cuisine makes them very popular around the world. Try these authentic Pakistani dishes and see which one becomes your favorite in the long run.

Author's Afterthoughts

Thanks ever so much to each of my cherished readers for investing the time to read this book!

I know you could have picked from many other books, but you chose this one. So, a big thanks for downloading this book and reading all the way to the end.

If you enjoyed this book or received value from it, I'd like to ask you for a favor. Please take a few minutes to post an honest and heartfelt review on Amazon.com. Your support does make a difference and helps to benefit other people.

Thanks for your Reviews!

Rachael Rayner